W9-BSV-372

- 2007

Artists at Work
Glass

Cheryl Jakab

Smart Apple Media

Smart Apple Media
2140 Howard Drive West
North Mankato
Minnesota 56003

First published in 2006 by
MACMILLAN EDUCATION AUSTRALIA PTY LTD
627 Chapel Street, South Yarra, Australia 3141

Visit our Web site at www.macmillan.com.au

Associated companies and representatives throughout the world.

Library of Congress Cataloging-in-Publication Data

Jakab, Cheryl.
    Glass / by Cheryl Jakab.
    p. cm.—(Artists at work)
    Includes index.
    ISBN-13: 978-1-58340-760-8
    1. Glassware—Juvenile literature. I. Title.

    NK5104.2.J25 2006
    748—dc22   2005057885

Edited by Sam Munday
Text and cover design by Karen Young
Page layout by Karen Young
Photo research by Jes Senbergs
Illustrations by Ann Likhovetsky

Printed in USA

Acknowledgments

The author would like to acknowledge and thank all the working artists and hobbyists who have been quoted, appear, or assisted in creating this book.

The author and the publisher are grateful to the following for permission to reproduce copyright material:

Cover photograph: American lampwork artist, Mark Hamilton, courtesy of Mark Hamilton.

Art Archive, pp. 15, 27; AusGlass, p. 24 (top); Gary Beecham, p. 5 (bottom); Persian Window, 1999 (glass), Chihuly, Dale (b.1941)/ © Delaware Art Museum, Wilmington, USA/Bridgeman Art Library, p. 22; Coo-ee Picture Library, pp. 6, 9; Corbis, pp. 7, 8, 12, 13 (all), 14, 16, 17, 18, 19; Rob Cruse, pp. 4 (right), 10 (bottom); Addison Doty, Flo Perkins, p. 11 (both); Glass Art, p. 24 (bottom); Mark Hamilton, p. 10 (top); Cheryl Jakab, pp. 23, 26; Lochman Transparencies, pp. 5 (top), 25; Lonely Planet Images, p. 4 (left); Photolibrary.com, p. 20; Wathaurong, p. 21 (both).

While every care has been taken to trace and acknowledge copyright, the publisher tenders their apologies for any accidental infringement where copyright has proved untraceable. Where the attempt has been unsuccessful, the publisher welcomes information that would redress the situation.

Please note

At the time of printing, the Internet addresses appearing in this book were correct. Owing to the dynamic nature of the Internet, however, we cannot guarantee that all these addresses will remain correct.

Contents

Glossary words

When a word is printed in **bold**, you can look up its meaning in the Glossary on page 31.

Glass artists

Look at these different artworks made by glass artists. Glass artists are people who design and make artworks out of glass. Glass artists make glass into a wide variety of items including:

- ◉ fine jewelry
- ◉ colored sculpted forms
- ◉ stained glass windows
- ◉ **glazed mosaics**
- ◉ cut and **etched** glass doors and vessels

▼ Jewelry is a popular kind of glass artwork.

◀ Glass sculptures are smooth to the touch.

> Many colored glass pieces make up a stained glass window.

Using glass

Glass artists are people who are very skilled at creating, choosing, and using glass. Glass can be used to produce many different effects. Glass art objects shine with color and can take complicated shapes.

In this book, you will find the answers to these questions and more:

- ⊙ What does a glass artist do?

- ⊙ What do glass artists need to know about glass to use it creatively?

- ⊙ How does glass help the artist express their ideas?

- ⊙ What do glass artists like about glass as a **medium** for art?

"I approach glass as a three-dimensional transparent canvas that I can form in any desired shape."
Gary Beecham, glass artist

⊙ Gary Beecham, a glass artist, at work.

What is glass?

Glass is a hard, but **brittle** mineral material. At room temperature, glass smashes easily when hit or dropped. When heated, glass melts and can be formed into almost any shape. When cooled, it is a very strong, stable, long-lasting substance. It does not react with materials that come into contact with it.

Glass can be **transparent**, **translucent**, or **opaque** depending on the ingredients used to make it. Glass is colored by adding particular chemicals when it is **molten**.

△ Different ingredients added to molten glass can produce different colors.

Ingredients of glass

The main ingredients in glass are silica crystals, which are the transparent grains in a handful of sand. The common name for rocks of silica crystals is quartz.

Formation of glass

Glass forms when silica is heated to very high temperatures (around 2,732°F). It becomes molten glass which is liquid, like thick honey. When it cools, the glass becomes solid.

Sand   Soda ash   Heat   Glass

The Artist Speaks

"A wonderful natural glass rock found in nature is called obsidian. It forms in the heat of volcanoes. We make glass by heating silica in **kilns** to form glass in a process similar to nature."
Jo Fraser, lampglass worker

🔺 This arrowhead is made of natural glass rock, called obsidian.

Glass work

Artists who work with glass use many different techniques. They can:

- ▶ create glass in very hot kilns
- ▶ shape hot glass by blowing or using molds
- ▶ color glass by adding chemicals
- ▶ use glazes to coat surfaces in glass
- ▶ reheat glass to reshape it
- ▶ work pieces of glass into patterns
- ▶ create glass beads

▼ Glassblowers work with molten glass from very hot kilns.

Shaping glass

Glass needs to be hot to be shaped. Heated glass melts to a liquid at different temperatures depending on the type of glass. The amount of soda in the glass varies the time it takes to **solidify**, giving the glassworker time to work the glass.

Two common ways of handling molten glass are by blowing, called "hot glass" working, and slumping, known as "cold glass" working.

▲ Slumped glass workers take formed glass and reheat it until it slumps into shape.

The slumping process

The basic slumping process has five main stages:

1. Heating—heating glass to the temperature when it slumps

2. Soaking—the temperature is maintained at maximum for a period of time

3. Rapid cooling—the temperature is dropped

4. Annealing—the temperature is held to make the glass less brittle

5. Cool to room temperature—the glass gradually becomes cool enough to touch and work

Glass artists today

Glass artists make use of all the techniques developed by others working with glass over thousands of years. They are also developing new ways to work with glass.

Lampwork

Lampwork involves reworking existing glass, generally to produce beads, toys, and figurines. Rods of glass are reheated by gas flames and reshaped by hand or machine. Lampworkers use a special torch to heat the glass rods, which can create small decorative items and jewelry.

Mosaics

Artists can also work pieces of glass or glazed tiles with a glassy surface to create pictures called mosaics. The art of mosaic creation is not new. Many ancient cultures made mosaics, some of which can still be seen today.

◀ Glazed tile mosaics create a long-lasting, colorful surface.

Glass as an artist's medium

Glass is both delicate and strong. It can be worked into fine detail and shaped into huge objects. Glass artists like the way that light passing through glass can be made into a wide range of colors. Most of all, artists like the fact that molten glass can be shaped and then solidifies very quickly.

The Artist Speaks

"I began to realize how flowers bud, bloom, and collapse, and how that related directly to the technical process of blowing glass—the bubble, the opening, and the folding."
**Flo Perkins,
glass artist**

◀ ▲ Glass can be used to create almost any shape, as shown in this glass cactus by Flo Perkins.

Glassblowing

Glassblowing is a widely-used technique. It involves shaping glass at high temperatures when the glass is molten.

The glass worker collects a small amount of molten glass, called a **gather**, on the end of a long pipe. The glass is rolled against a steel table (this process is called **mavering**) and allowed to cool slightly. The artist then blows into the pipe to create a bubble of molten glass. The artist continues to work on the shape, reheating the glass regularly. Tools such as tongs and paddles are also used to help form the shape.

When the shape is finished, a glass rod called a punty is attached to the bottom. The piece is then broken off the blowpipe, and the join is heated and smoothed. The artist then breaks the punty off and the piece is cooled.

▼ The punty is used to help form the glass artwork, but is removed before the piece is finished.

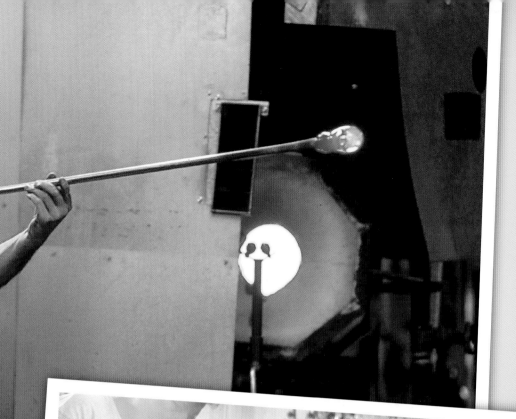

🔺 The gather gets bigger the harder the artist blows.

Shaping blown glass

Shapes and patterns can be created in blown glass using molds.
This can be done before or after blowing by placing the gather in a mold. The shaped gather is then blown or pressed to the desired size. Stems, handles, or feet are formed by applying more gathers. Color can be added to a blown glass bubble by dipping it into molten glass of a different color. This is called "flashing."

🔺 This gather is being shaped by pressing.

Glass history

Glassmaking was discovered about 5,000 years ago, probably by accident. Perhaps a fire lit on a beach turned some of the sand into glass beads? Glass first appeared as beads but people soon developed techniques to produce bowls, jars, and vases.

Glassmaking history has five main periods:

1. Early glassmaking is developed (3000 B.C.)

2. Glassblowing technique is invented by the ancient Romans (around 50 B.C.)

3. Glassmaking skills take time to spread through Europe (400–1100 B.C.)

4. Glassmaking skills, especially Venetian skills, develop and spread (1400s)

5. Modern **mass-produced** everyday glass becomes common (1800s).

◀ This glass bottle was recovered from the ancient city of Aphrodisias in Turkey.

⬤ These Phoenician glass vessels are fine examples of early glassblowing.

Great glass traditions

Early civilizations in Egypt and Mesopotamia were the first to use glass to make objects. These first glassworkers carved items from solid blocks of glass. At this stage, some wealthy people may even have had glass in windows. For thousands of years glass was a luxury, available only to the very rich.

Glassblowing was invented around 50 B.C. During the 1100s, glassmaking became popular in Europe after being ignored for around 700 years. Stained glass windows from that time can still be seen in some churches today.

Phoenician glassmakers

Of all the early glassworkers, the greatest were the ancient Phoenicians. The Phoenicians came up with the technique of glassblowing that is still used today by glass artists. Glassworking had been known for nearly 1,500 years before the Phoenicians invented this method.

Glass treasures

A large range of glass techniques, colors, and forms have been produced over time. Perhaps the greatest glass treasures from the past are ancient Chinese glass and medieval stained glass.

Chinese glass

▼ These three miniature glass bottles are perfect examples of Chinese glass from the Qing Dynasty.

Chinese glass is produced by covering a white glass vessel in a layer of red glass. Some of the red glass is then carved away to make patterns. The best examples show detailed scenes of Chinese life from the Qing Dynasty (particularly between 1736 and 1796).

Stained glass

Stained glass is colored glass used in windows. The pieces of glass are held in strips of lead in a metal framework. Stained glass looks best with light coming through it, so is sometimes known as "painting with light." The best examples were produced in France from around 1130 to 1330.

The Crystal Palace

The Crystal Palace was one of the most amazing buildings ever imagined. The clear, almost colorless glass that we know so well today was first developed in the 1400s. By the 1800s clear glass was being mass-produced. Techniques had improved to the point where whole buildings could be made of glass.

The Crystal Palace was the first and perhaps the most spectacular glass building. It was a huge hall made for the Great Exhibition of 1851 in London, England. It is said to be the first piece of modern architecture.

It was made up of 300,000 sheets of glass on an iron frame. After the exhibition, the building was dismantled and then rebuilt in South London. The Crystal Palace was destroyed by fire in 1936.

▲ No other building in the world was like the Crystal Palace when it was first built.

CASE STUDY
Murano glass

Venice in Italy has a long history of glassmaking. Glassmaking skills declined after the fall of the Roman Empire around 400 A.D. The city of Venice, however, remained a glass-making center and maintained the skills which were lost in other areas. In 1292, Venice isolated glassmaking to the island of Murano. This was to protect other buildings from fires commonly started in glassworks.

Murano glass masters have produced some of the finest traditional Venetian glasswork ever made. Their glassmakers continue the Venetian glass traditions from Roman times to this day.

▶ This crystal glass pitcher was made in Murano in the 1800s.

🔺 Murano glass artworks are made by hand and can be very decorative.

Throughout the 1900s, new glassblowing techniques were developed. By the 1930s some Italian glassworkers, including those at Murano, had introduced new design ideas to produce new glass styles. They started to explore ways of changing the temperatures at which glass could be worked. Glass with higher amounts of soda solidifies slowly, creating what is known as "slow glass." Murano glassworkers used this method for sculpture.

For around 2,000 years glassblowing had been used mainly to create bowls, cups, glasses, and so on. During the 1950s this changed, and blown glass was used to make large sculptural artworks.

Where glass artists work

Glass artists need a studio or workshop and many tools to make their art. These can be expensive. Glass artists who make hot or warm glass artworks have their own small glass kiln in their workshop. Lampwork glass artists only require a gas flame to be able to work their rods of glass.

Studio glass

During the 1960s, glass artists began to build their own studios containing their own glass kilns. This became known as the "studio glass" movement. Until this time most hot glass artists created designs that were then made in factories by workers.

The Artist Speaks

"My decisions are made at the time of creation, in the heat of the moment at the furnace."
**Harvey Littleton,
glass artist**

◀ Glass artists need specialist equipment in their workshop.

CASE STUDY
Wathaurong Glass

The Wathaurong Glass company was formed to express Indigenous Australian art in a non-traditional material—glass. Many techniques are used by the glassworkers including the use of **kiln forming** and sand etching. Artworks that have been produced include windows, platters, bowls, and tabletops. The Wathaurong (wathawurrung or wada warrung) peoples consist of 25 clans from around Geelong in Victoria, Australia.

▲ Wathaurong glass artist Byron Edwards.

◀ Painted slump glass, titled "Bunjil's Creation," by Byron Edwards.

Showing glass artworks

Like all artists, glassworkers need to display and sell their works. Glass items look particularly attractive when displayed well. Glass displays in galleries and shops are well-lit so the transparency, colors, and shape can stand out. Glass artworks must be displayed carefully in public, as they are extremely fragile pieces.

Some major glass artworks are made especially to stand in public spaces, rather than being exhibited in galleries. This is a fabulous opportunity for the artist, as many people will be able to see their work. These kinds of artworks are made of strong glass so they do not break.

▼ Using light in a display can make glass artworks stand out.

Making a living as an artist

Many glass artists produce a range of items made to the same pattern or design, known as production items. These production items use standard techniques and usually take less time to make than new designs. The sale of production items such as drinking glasses, jewelry, vases, or platters is important. It means that the artist can afford to spend time on their more complicated artworks.

Jo Fraser creates glass artworks in her workshop. She also creates jewelry to sell as production items. The money from this allows her to work on her more artistic pieces that take longer to produce. Jo makes complex fused glass beads with detailed patterns to go into her more expensive works.

🔺 Jo Fraser working on a piece of jewelry.

The Artist Speaks

"After watching someone manipulate molten glass into a beautiful figurine ... I was hooked."
Chad Pitts, studio glassworker

23

Glass artists' groups

There are many glass artists' groups who share their work and ideas on the Internet. Individuals, groups, and associations display work, share ideas, deal with issues, and even sell items online. This sharing of ideas electronically has had a major effect on glass art. Many glass techniques that were being used by just a few groups are now available online for everyone to see. Ausglass and Glass Art are two examples that have online galleries showing the works of contemporary glass artists. This allows people to browse the best of international glasswork online.

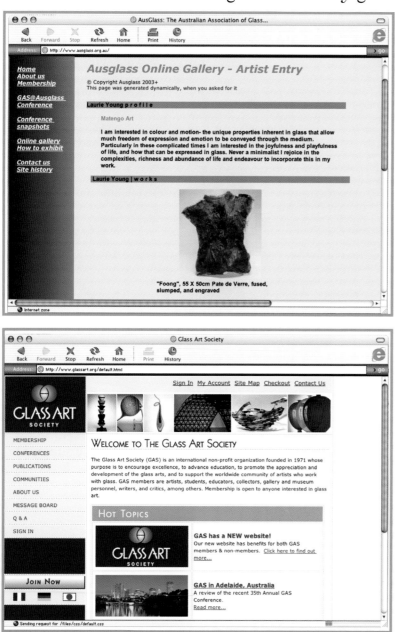

Issues for glass artists

Glass artists' groups are useful for viewing and showing artworks. They can also be very helpful in sharing information about issues surrounding glass artwork. These may include health and safety issues, or how their work might affect the environment.

◀ Online galleries can display artworks and information about the artist.

Health and safety

Every artist must be careful when working but particularly glassworkers. Working with hot glass furnaces and broken glass can be dangerous.

Most injuries can be prevented by using common sense. Glass artists should:

▶ never work in bare feet—they must wear shoes with covered toes

▶ tie back long hair

▶ wear close fitting clothes made of natural fibers

▶ wear long sleeves for protection when reaching into the kiln

▶ wear gloves and **respirators** when needed

Glassworkers and the environment

Some of Earth's natural **resources** are used to make glass, such as sand, and large amounts of energy used by kilns. Using too much of these natural resources can be harmful to the environment. Using **recycled** glass takes less energy than creating new glass and it also saves money.

CASE STUDY
Glass beadmaking

Glass beadmaking is an art, craft, and hobby that is increasing in popularity today. The basic technique of making beads by a process called lampwork is simple. Hot glass is wound around an iron bar, called a mandril. Lampwork is also called "wound work." The beadmaker turns the rod to build up the shape of the bead. The formed bead can then be decorated with lines, shapes, and raised areas in various colors of glass.

🔻 Glass beadmaking requires patience and a steady hand.

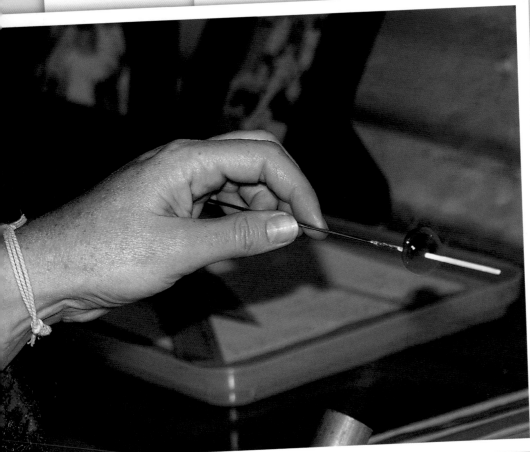

After the bead is formed, other materials such as gold can be added to it. The bead can also be etched or carved.

Glass beadmaker websites are a good place to start learning about working as a beadmaker. The International Society of Glass Beadmakers (www.isgb.org) has a great deal of information about the art.

Lampwork glass

Glass beads are made from lampwork glass which melts at lower temperatures than other glass. Lampwork glass comes in rods, in a huge variety of colors. The rods are grouped according to hardness. Each type of glass rod has different characteristics:

- ▶ Satake from Japan is soft and comes in a wide variety of colors

- ▶ Moretti from Italy is medium hard and is easily worked

- ▶ Bullseye, made in the United States of America, is available in a wide range of colors and can be used for fusing

- ▶ Dichrois, meaning "two-colored," has metal oxides that make it show off its colors

"I make my beads in sets. It feels more finished than one bead and tells a story."
Karen Leonardo, lampwork glass artist

🔺 This necklace was made from multicolored glass pearls in the 1930s at Murano, Italy.

PROJECT
Make a glass bead bracelet

Creating jewelry from beads requires careful selection of colors, shapes, and patterns. Selecting beads depends very much on the effect you want to create. You may want to vary the size, color, or transparency of the beads you use. This will help you create your own piece of artwork.

What you need:

- about 20 glass beads, or more if tiny

- good flexible wire for beading, about 1 inch (2.5 cm) longer than the bracelet will be

- wire crimps

- wire joiners

- flat-nose pliers

- flat-sided wire cutters

What to do:

1. Arrange the beads in a range of patterns in a white container to help you select a design.

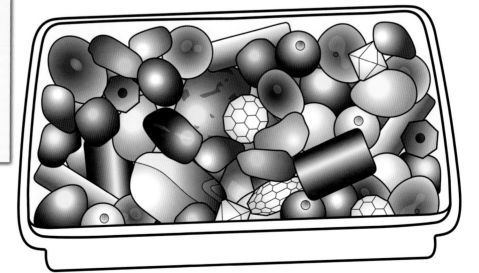

2. Thread the beads onto the wire, starting at the center bead and working outwards.

3. Complete one side before starting on the other.

4. Use the flat-nose pliers to add the wire crimps to hold the beads in place.

5. Add the wire joiners to join the ends of the bracelet and use the wire cutters to cut off any remaining wire.

Glass timeline

B.C.

3000 Glassmaking process discovered, first known made glass in Middle East

1500 Large-scale glassmaking of earliest known glass vessels made in Mesopotamia

300 Mold pressing of glass used by Greeks

50 Glass blowpipe first used

A.D.

1100s Stained glass introduced

1300s Crown glass used to make clear flat window glass

1400s Clear glass first made by Venetian glassworkers

1600s Flat plate glass produced—molten glass poured on an iron table to create large sheets

1880s Glass began to be mass produced

1884 The Jena glassworks in Germany produced toughened glass that was less sensitive to heat by adding the chemical boron silicate

1909 Safety glass (glass that does not shatter) produced by placing a sheet of celluloid between two sheets of glass

1918 Continuous sheets of window glass produced in flat sheets

1952 Float glass, made by floating hot glass on a surface, produced flat sheets much more cheaply than previous methods

1960 Studio glassmaking began

late 1900s Bulletproofing of glass developed

Glossary

brittle does not bend, easily shattered

etched carved and cut

gather the hot molten glass collected onto a blowpipe

glazed a glassy cover or finish

kiln forming shaped using the heat from a kiln

kilns furnaces or ovens used to process materials at high temperatures

mass-produced produced on large scale

mavering shaping of molten glass

medium material used

molten in a melted liquid form

mosaics artworks made up from many small pieces of glass

opaque does not allow light to pass through

recycled used again by reprocessing

resources things people make use of

respirators safety equipment worn over the mouth to keep from breathing in dust

solidify turn to a solid

translucent semi-transparent, allows some light to pass through

transparent allows light to pass through

Index